The Sky Ladder

Written by Nancy O'Connor

Illustrated by Kim Woolley

Flying Start
to Literacy®

Contents

Chapter 1

A new school year

Mei Li giggled with her friend Wu as they ate their lunch of rice and vegetables. "Did you see that boy's drawing?" Wu asked. "It looked like the scarecrow in my father's field."

"Hush, Teacher Lin is coming," Mei Li whispered. She lowered her eyes and bent her head over her food.

Mei Li was glad to be back in school, even if it meant being away from her family for weeks at a time. Her family lived in a small village at the top of a mountain. The land was so precious to the farmers that there was no room to build a school. The only one nearby was in the valley, down a sheer cliff face.

And the only way for anyone from the mountaintop village to reach the school or the city was by climbing a series of steep ladders.

Mei Li loved her family very much, but during the summer break, she rose at dawn every day to help her father pick walnuts or dig potatoes. By midday, she was exhausted and soaked in sweat. In the afternoon, she helped her mother with chores. It was hard work.

Mei Li's father was a farmer, like most of the men in their village. If he was lucky, he might earn a dollar a day selling his potatoes, chili peppers and walnuts in the city.

Once a week, he would make the long and difficult journey down the mountain, carrying his goods on his back. Shopkeepers often demanded low prices because they knew the farmers would not want to carry their unsold goods back to the top of the mountain.

Mei Li's mother took care of her baby sister, Bao. She also cooked, kept the house tidy and cared for the family's animals. Their home was simple, with only two beds and a cooking fire. When they ate their meals, they sat on a rug on the dirt floor. During the cold winter, their pigs and chickens shared the house.

Although the hours at school were long and the teachers strict, Mei Li enjoyed the learning. Now that she was nine, she and the other four students her age had begun English lessons. In just the first two weeks of school, she had learnt to recognise all the numerals and how to count to twenty in the new language. There was one thing she still hated, however – calisthenics. First thing every morning, the students all gathered in the schoolyard to exercise. Even before the sun was up! *Ayyy!*

Teacher Lin clapped his hands to get everyone's attention. "Finish your lunch," he said. "It is time for rest."

Wu and Mei Li obediently finished their last bites and then went inside to place their empty bowls on the bench. As they lined up, Mei Li noticed one of the new students, a boy named Chen. His bowl was still full of food.

"Are you finished, Chen?" she asked him quietly. The teachers did not like food to be wasted.

"I am not hungry," he whispered.

Chen's family and Mei Li's were neighbours. He was only six and this was his first time at the boarding school. During the past two weeks, she had often heard him crying in bed at night. She, too, had been homesick when she first started school.

"Are you sick?" she asked. He shook his head. "Then what's wrong?"

"I miss my mother and father," he said.

"We all miss our families," Mei Li said, "but you will soon get used to living at school. And, anyway, we will be going home to see them on Friday."

"But I am mostly afraid of the sky ladder." Chen began to cry.

Chapter 2

The dangerous sky ladder

From the bottom of the valley, it seemed to the children that the ladder reached all the way to the sky. The ladder was almost one kilometre long, and the climb was dangerous for everyone, but especially for the children. That is why the students lived at the school and went home only for a weekend visit every two weeks.

Mei Li shuddered when she remembered the old ladders. They had been made of bamboo tied together with ropes made of twisted vines. Some of them were one hundred years old. The climb took over two hours. She had cried many times as she clambered up and down them. But finally, her leg and arm muscles grew stronger, and she overcame her fear.

"Don't be such a baby!" Wu said crossly to Chen. "You should be glad that the new ladder is made of steel. They were much more dangerous before. Many people fell to their deaths." The little boy's eyes grew wide.

It was true that people had died, but Mei Li still glared at her friend. "Don't be so mean, Wu. You know that even some adults are afraid of them."

Two years earlier, a newspaper reporter had come to the school because he had heard about the sky ladder and the most recent death that had occurred. He and a photographer followed the students up the mountain on their trek home.

The photographer had sobbed when she looked at the steep cliff and rickety old ladders. She asked if there was another way to get to the top. The children had laughed. One boy, who Mei Li thought was rude, had said, "We would go another way if there was one!"

A short time later, the news people had their article about the sky ladder published in the newspaper. The readers grew angry when they read how dangerous the trek was for the village children, so the government agreed to build the steel ladder. There was even talk these days of building a cable car and bringing tourists to visit the school and village. How Mei Li would love to ride in a cable car!

"Stop daydreaming and hurry up," Wu said. "Teacher Lin is waiting for us."

Mei Li hid Chen's bowl of uneaten food at the back of the bench. "Wu, don't you remember being afraid when you were six?" she asked. Then she took the small boy by the hand and walked with him to the sleeping room. "He is worried, just like we used to be."

"Well, he'd better get over it," Wu said. "It's almost Friday."

Chapter 3
Friday arrives

Two days later at lunch, Mei Li sought out Chen and sat down beside him. Wu made a face, but she joined her friend anyway.

"Tell me what you are looking forward to when you get home, Chen," Mei Li said. "I can almost taste my mother's chili pepper chicken and buckwheat pancakes. They are my favourite foods!"

Chen sat silently, playing with his lunch.

"For me, it's my mother's dumplings," Wu said. "I dreamt about them last night. Dozens of dumplings were floating above my bed." She laughed, which made Chen smile.

Finally, he spoke. "We have six chickens. They give us many eggs. I like when my mother makes rice with eggs and vegetables."

"Okay," said Mei Li, "think about that yummy rice and eggs when we are climbing home this afternoon. What else makes you happy?"

"When my mother sings to me," he said.

"What song does she sing?" Mei Li asked. Chen began to sing it softly.

Mei Li nodded and hummed along. "I often sing to myself while I climb. It helps me take my mind off of the danger."

When they had finished lunch, all the students went to the sleeping room to collect their schoolbooks and homework. They put them in their backpacks, then gathered in the play area and formed a line. Mei Li held Chen's hand. Wu joined them. It was almost time for the helping fathers to begin the trek home.

"My father told me he could not come to take me home today," Chen said. "He is selling our potatoes in the market."

"Mine is also at the market," Mei Li said. "Some Fridays, our fathers can come. Other Fridays, they can't."

"He told me to be brave, even though I would be alone, but I am not brave."

"Well, you are not alone." Mei Li smiled at Chen. "You've got me."

The fathers led the way out of the schoolyard. The older boys and girls spaced themselves in between the younger ones. Chen followed Wu, and Mei Li followed him. Everyone chatted about their plans for the weekend as they made their way along the shady, dirt path towards the base of the cliff. Golden monkeys screeched from the treetops as they passed by.

Suddenly, something dropped out of a tree overhead onto Wu's back. She began screaming and hopping from foot to foot.

"What is it? What is it?" she cried. "Get it off me!" She slapped frantically at her hair and shoulders.

Chen ran up to her and said, "Bend down. It is only a tree dragon." Wu crouched in the path, and Chen put his hands gently around the big lizard. "You don't need to be afraid. It only eats grasshoppers and other insects, not people."

Everyone laughed.

"I guess everyone is afraid of something," Mei Li said to her friend.

"Don't be such a baby, Wu," one of the older boys said.

Wu's face was red when she stood up. She smiled weakly at the group standing around her. "It just surprised me. That's the only reason I screamed."

Chen turned to Mei Li. "Can you open my backpack? I want to put the tree dragon in so I can take him home. They make very good pets."

Once the lizard was safely zipped in with Chen's homework, the group headed out again for the base of the cliff.

Chapter 4

Climbing to the sky

The ladder's metal rungs and side rails gleamed in the afternoon sunlight. Chen squeezed Mei Li's hand. When she looked down at him, his eyes were watering. "Don't cry," she said quickly. "Think about your tree dragon, and your rice and eggs, and remember to sing your favourite song. Those things will take your mind off being afraid."

"Okay," Chen said, sniffling.

"Be sure not to look down," Mei Li said. "Look up at Wu instead." Wu put her foot on the first rung and began to climb.

"Now you," Mei Li said to Chen. She boosted him up. "Keep your hands dry." She followed her friends.

One step, two steps, three steps . . . eighteen, nineteen, twenty. Mei Li counted each step aloud in English as she climbed.

"Okay, the first ladder is finished," Wu said over her shoulder. "Only sixteen more to go." She stepped carefully along the path across the cliff face to the next ladder and started climbing again. The melody of a children's rhyming song floated down from above, and she smiled. She had learnt that song, too, when she was a first-year student. Mei Li began to hum along, and Chen joined in.

Suddenly, Chen's foot slipped off the rung above Mei Li. His shoe hit her in the face, right on the bridge of her nose. She gasped in pain and surprise, but she did not let go.

"Ayieee! I'm going to fall!" Chen screamed.

Everyone stopped. The father nearest them shouted. "Do you need help?"

Mei Li took a deep breath. Chen's scream had startled her, and she felt the beginning of a headache, but she called out, "No, no, we're okay." Then she patted the little boy above her on the back of his leg. "You're not going to fall," she assured him.

"I'm sorry I kicked you," Chen said. "My legs feel so shaky."

"You are doing great. Remember what Wu said – don't look down."

They had been climbing for more than an hour, and the sun began to drop behind the mountain. Parts of the path were in shadow. The metal rungs of the ladder no longer felt warm. Although she was tired, Mei Li found that worrying about Chen took her mind off her exhaustion. She encouraged him at the bottom of each new ladder and chattered to him about her baby sister and the food that would be waiting when they got home.

"Look up there, Chen." She took one hand off the ladder and quickly pointed skywards. "The last one!"

"Good. I'm very tired," he said, but she saw that he was smiling.

"I can smell the cooking fires now," Wu called down. "My mouth is ready for those dumplings!"

Chapter 5

Home, finally!

One of the fathers stood at the top of the cliff and bent down to pull the children up as they reached the last rung.

"Good job," he said, and gave each one a pat on the shoulder before they ran off to their waiting families.

When Mei Li reached the top of the climb, she saw Wu talking to Chen. She heard her say, "Thank you for saving me from that fierce tree dragon. I guess everyone acts like a baby once in a while. I just don't like lizards, especially when they surprise me and jump on my back."

Chen laughed. "That's okay." Then he raced off to meet his mother.

When Mei Li spied her own mother, holding Bao, she ran to her. She kissed her sister on her round, pink cheek then hugged her mother.

"Guess what we are having for dinner," her mother said.

"Could it be chili pepper chicken and buckwheat pancakes?" Mei Li asked. She and her mother played this same guessing game every time Mei Li came home, and the answer was always the same. "I will help you cook," she said, taking Mother's hand.

Soon, Mei Li's father arrived home, tired from his long trip to the market in the city. But he was in good spirits. He asked Mei Li how she was doing in school. An education and good grades were important to her parents. Just as she started to tell him all the English she had learnt, there was a knock on the door.

When Mother opened it, Chen stood there, holding a bundle of cloth in his hands.

"Hello, Chen. How are you?"

"Fine, thank you. Here is a gift." He stretched out his hands. Mei Li's mother took the bundle and opened it. Inside were four warm brown eggs.

"What are these for?" Mother asked.

"Mei Li helped me climb the sky ladder today. It was my first time by myself. She made me brave. My family wants to thank her."

Mei Li stepped up beside her mother. "The sky ladder will get easier every time you climb it, I promise. And even though I don't like them, those exercises every morning make your muscles strong. Hey – how is your tree dragon?"

"He has already eaten a cockroach," Chen replied. "I couldn't find any grasshoppers." Then he laughed and scampered off into the night.

Mei Li's father looked at her, then smiled and put his arm around her. "It is wonderful that you helped Chen. Your mother and I are proud of our kind daughter."

A note from the author

This story is based on fact. The tiny village of Atule'er
is located on a mountaintop in the Sichuan province of
southwestern China. Only four hundred people live there.
Twice a month the village children risk their lives to get to
school because they want an education.

Things improved in 2016 when the old bamboo and vine
ladders were replaced with metal. However, the construction
was very challenging. Workers had to carry 1,500 heavy
pipes up the mountain strapped on their backs. But the
ladders finally reached the top – 800 metres high! Now with
side rails and sturdier rungs, it is a bit safer for the children
to get to school and their parents to get to the market in the
nearest town several kilometres away.